# Invisible
# Bridges

*Books by John Ullmen, Ph.D. and Melissa Karz, MBA*

Invisible Bridges for Teens

Invisible Bridges for Kids

*Also by John Ullmen, Ph.D.*

Don't Kill the Bosses: Escaping the Hierarchy Trap
(coauthored with Sam Culbert)

# Invisible Bridges

Building
Professional Relationships
For Results

## John Ullmen, Ph.D.
### and
## Melissa Karz, MBA

For More Information About
Invisible Bridges
Learning Materials, Workbooks, Audio CDs, Assessments, Seminars
310.266.1559
www.priconnect.com

# CONTENTS

*Invisible Bridges* is a brief and powerful story that demonstrates the principles and practices of relationship building in professional life. The characters are imaginary, but their adventures represent challenges and opportunities all of us face.

As the story opens, one of the characters confronts a question about what he should do next. He has pursued an important goal with passion and hard work, but he keeps coming up short. He gets some advice that sets him on a new course.

As the story unfolds, the characters find themselves in surprising and amusing situations, and along the way, they reveal enduring truths about how to build and maintain professional relationships.

The story is based on extensive research into what it takes to build strong, trusting relationships and networks. For years, Ullmen and Karz have studied managers, executives, and professionals from different industries, cultures, and types of organizations. Through this story, they weave their findings into action tools that anyone can remember and use long afterward.

People from all types of organizations and at any stage in their professional lives can enjoy the story and put its insights into action immediately and for the rest of their careers.

The authors would like to acknowledge Spencer Johnson, MD for the inspiration to share their findings on building professional relationships in the form of a story.

We would also like to thank others who have offered feedback on the manuscript, including Jim and Emily Adcox, Dwayne Benefield, Tony Drockton, Alan Guno, Mel Hall, Stephanie Kagimoto, Freita Keluche, Tom Rubinson, Glenn and Diane Rupert, Ron and Alexandra Seigel, James "Sully" Sullivan, and Tom Zelenovic.

Special thanks to Cris Sumbi for her editing and Libby Gill for her advice.

## Introduction:
## A Familiar Discussion

AT a company meeting, the CEO issued a challenge to his people: "To meet the threat from competitors, we need to get better at relationship building, both inside and outside of our organization. I want to hear your best ideas on how we can do it."

Later a group of executives and managers from different business units gathered to discuss the matter.

Frank from Operations said, "I'm glad our CEO brought up relationships within the company. It's crucial for our Operations group, and we're having trouble. It seems like we're always running into conflicts with other parts of the organization, which makes it hard to keep things running on time."

"I agree," said Sharon from Marketing. "We say we want to be collaborative, but we act as if we work in silos. We don't cooperate, and we protect our territory."

"I suppose it makes sense in a way," said Frank. "It's about survival. Everyone competes for headcount and budget. You've got to make sure your group has what it needs or else you'll fail."

"But if we're doing that across the company as a whole," Sharon continued, "then we're all in trouble, especially if other companies are figuring out how to avoid it."

James from Information Technology said, "We have relationship problems too because we get caught in the middle. Every group tells us *their* project is most important, and they expect us to do it quickly and perfectly. We're trying to balance everyone's interests, and still we get criticized from all sides. It's frustrating."

Rebecca from Sales chimed in, "Sales faces a similar balancing act with clients outside the organization. Just like you, James, we don't have authority over the people we're dealing with—in fact, it's just the opposite. The clients keep us all in business. We've got to satisfy their needs and build their trust and confidence, but we also have to negotiate firmly and keep costs down. It gets really hard when we can't do what they want within budget and we have to say no to them."

Steve from Finance said, "We've done the team-building programs, communication workshops, and customer service activities across the company. They've been helpful, but we still have more progress to make. I wonder if there is anything else we can do."

Sharon turned to Gordon, a key account executive. "You have a great reputation in this company for building relationships, both inside the company and with clients. Does it come easily for you?"

Gordon laughed. "I wish it was easy. To tell you the truth, I had big problems with relationships earlier in my career. I thought I was much better at it than I actually was, and I almost got fired."

The others looked shocked. Gordon continued, "It's true. I was focused on delivering results, and I thought that relationships would take care of themselves. It became clear I was wrong when I missed being promoted from Senior Manager to Director the first time. I was stunned."

"What happened?" asked Frank.

"Well," Gordon said, "my boss told me, 'Gordon, you're the hardest worker I've got, and maybe the smartest too, about your area of business. But you've reached a level where your own efforts and expertise aren't enough.'

"He went on to say I needed the support of others from different parts of the organization, and I wasn't getting it. Not only that but if the trend continued, he'd have no choice but to let me go."

"How did things change for you?" asked Sharon.

"I realized I was in trouble, so I asked him for advice. It seemed like a good place to start because he got great performance results, and he was also excellent at all that relationship stuff—communicating, handling conflict, building trust.

"What did he say?" asked James.

"He told me a story," said Gordon. "I thought it was strange because the story had animals in it, like a fable. At first I thought it was a joke, but then I started to listen. As the story went on, I started to see myself in it. I know it sounds goofy, but the story was a real turning point for me."

"Tell us the story," said Rebecca.

"Oh, I don't know," Gordon said. "Are you sure you want to hear it? I mean, the main character is a gopher."

"You can't set it up like that and not tell it!" exclaimed Frank.

"All right," Gordon said. And so he began.

*The Story*

## Chapter I:
## An Ordinary and Extraordinary Gopher

GARY was an ordinary gopher in every way but one: he wanted to fly.

Gary worked hard every day digging his gopher tunnels. And at every day's end, he climbed out from his tunnel and watched the birds sail through the sky high above. He told his friend Beaver, "What a feeling it must be to soar in the air. I wish I could do it and see what's it's like to be up there."

One day, Gary got an idea. He excitedly gathered feathers from the ground, and when Beaver asked him what he was doing, Gary said to come watch him fly. Beaver was skeptical, but he went along with his friend.

Gary's idea was to use the feathers like the birds do. He held a feather in each of his front paws, stood up on his hind legs, and began running. Actually it wasn't much of a run; it was more of a waddle.

Trotting awkwardly along a few steps, Gary waved the feathers up and down, but then he lost his balance. He stumbled and pitched forward. "Whoooa!" he exclaimed, lost his grip on the feathers, then turned a somersault, and ended up with a feather stuck crosswise in his mouth.

Beaver tried not to laugh, but he couldn't help himself. He bent down to where Gary sat, cupped his hands to his mouth, and shouted as if speaking to someone up in the sky, "How's the view up there?"

"Pffew!" Gary spat the feather out. He looked annoyed for a moment, but then he laughed too.

"I know what the problem is," Gary said. "I need to start from a higher spot. If I get a start in the air, then I'll be able to flap like the birds and stay aloft."

"And how are you going to start from a higher spot?" asked Beaver.

"I'll walk to the edge of Mossy Cliff with my feathers, then jump off," said Gary.

"Hmmm," said Beaver, realizing that his friend's enthusiasm was clouding his judgment. "That's a creative idea Gary, but—"

"But what?" asked Gary.

"But . . . it's dumb. That cliff is a hundred feet high. But you made me think of something else that might be safe to try."

"What's that?" asked Gary.

"Come to the riverbank and I'll show you," said Beaver.

When they arrived, Beaver showed Gary a tree nearby with a branch that reached out over the water. The branch was a couple of feet above the river, and Beaver pointed out how Gary could walk out on the branch and jump from there. "A splash landing is better than a crash landing," he said.

"Oh, so you don't think it will work? Ha! You'll see." Gary marched up to the tree, but his plump belly made climbing a challenge. Gary turned to Beaver sheepishly. "Uh, Beaver," he said, "can you give me a boost?"

Beaver hoisted Gary onto his shoulders and lifted him onto the low-hanging branch. "See you in a couple of hours, Beaver!" said Gary. Then he lifted his arms, flapped his feathers, and jumped.

Up Gary went into the air, almost an inch, and down Gary plopped into the water. He bobbed up and sneezed twice. Beaver reached out and helped him back to shore.

"Cheer up," said Beaver. "It wasn't much of a flight, but it was a respectable belly flop for a little guy."

"Sure, sure, go ahead and laugh," said Gary. "But it could have worked if the breeze was stronger."

"I agree," said Beaver, "if the breeze was a typhoon."

Gary patted his plump belly, then flexed his little arms. "Are you saying this lean, mean flying machine isn't aerodynamic?"

"Lean and mean is not enough," said Beaver. "You'll need more power to make those feathers work like wings."

Gary saw that Beaver was right and resolved that next time he would tie the feathers to his arms. He sketched out a new design in the sand. "This way my arms will stay straight and secure. I'll be just like a bird, flapping my wings."

Beaver picked up a little piece of tree bark from the ground and said, "Yes, and if you tie this piece of bark to your nose, you can call it a beak. Then you'd be even more like a bird." Beaver held the bark up to Gary's nose, pretending to be helpful.

"Very funny," said Gary. He followed the flight of a passing butterfly, watching longingly as it ascended a nearby tree. "I really want to fly, Beaver. I wish I could find a way."

"I've got to hand it to you," said Beaver. "When it comes to your goals, you are the hardest working, most persistent guy I know. I really admire that. And you're constantly coming up with new ideas to try."

"Yes, but nothing seems to work," Gary said.

"Hey, you should be proud of what you've done, Gary. I'll bet you've gone farther with flight than any gopher in history. You even flew a little off that branch, technically speaking. You went up at least an inch."

Gary kicked the dirt with his foot. "That wasn't so much flying as falling."

"With style though!" said Beaver. "Maybe you're looking at it the wrong way, Gary. It's more about trying than flying. It's about giving your best. Somebody wise once said, 'It's not the end, it's the journey.'"

Gary laughed. "The end? It's not the end of the flight I'm having trouble with. It's the beginning and the middle. I barely begin, and I get no middle at all."

Beaver snapped his fingers. "That's a thought! You know what you need, Gary? A new beginning, a different perspective. And I've got someone in mind who will have just that. Follow me."

## Chapter II:

## An Old Fish and a New Direction

BEAVER trotted along the riverbank with Gary following close behind. A few minutes later, they came to a marshy area, and Beaver slipped into the water and slapped his tail on the surface quickly, three times. After a moment, the water parted, and to the surface came what can only be described as a very old fish.

"My friend, Beaver," he said, "to what do I owe the honor?"

"Old Fish, you're good at giving advice, and I think my friend here could use some advice right now. Gary, I'd like to introduce you to my friend, Old Fish.

"Thank you for the compliment, Beaver," said Old Fish. "A pleasure to meet you, Gary."

Beaver continued, "And Gary is extraordinary too. He's the only gopher I've ever heard of who wants to fly."

"I've never seen a gopher fly," said Old Fish.

"Neither have I," said Gary.

Beaver told Old Fish of the day's events and how hard Gary had worked for a long time to achieve his goal.

"Hmmm," said Old Fish. "I think I understand. There's something I wanted to achieve for years, but no matter how hard I tried, I couldn't get it done. Until one day—"

"Until one day what?" asked Gary. Beaver smiled.

Old Fish said, "Until one day I talked to a friend and made a breakthrough. May I offer you some advice?"

"Please," said Gary. "What do you suggest?"

Old Fish said there were two things. First, Gary should write down everything he learned from being with Beaver today as he tried to fly. Gary said that he didn't learn anything. He and Beaver just spent some time together as they often did. Old Fish said that nevertheless, Gary should give it some thought and write down what he discovered. He promised that what Gary learned would grow if he wrote about it. "But first," he said, "you have to keep track of it. Start with today. You'll discover more than you might imagine."

Gary thought about it for a moment. "Okay," said Gary, "I'll give it a try. What's the second thing?"

"The second thing," said Old Fish, "is a bigger challenge. Gary, you must help someone who is bigger, stronger, and faster than you are."

Gary was puzzled. He was expecting some helpful advice that would make his goal easier to achieve, and instead his life just got much more complicated. For one thing, he had to write things down when he had nothing to write about. In addition, he had not only one nearly impossible thing to do but two. On top of figuring out how to fly, he had to help someone bigger, stronger, and faster than he was.

"If they are bigger, stronger, and faster," asked Gary, "then what could they need from me? How about if I help someone small, weak, and slow instead?"

Old Fish laughed and said he wouldn't discourage Gary from helping anyone, but his advice was unchanged. "Bigger, stronger, faster," Old Fish repeated. "And they can be smarter too, no problem with that."

"Okay, okay," pleaded Gary. "I better get going before you make it even more impossible. If I can figure out how to do this, what then?"

"You'll see," said Old Fish, smiling as he paddled backward. "When the time comes, you'll figure out what to do next." He waved a fin and said, "I look forward to seeing you again, Gary."

Gary said goodbye to Old Fish and Beaver, and deep in thought, he walked toward home.

Gary considered what Old Fish told him to think about. What had he learned today when he was trying to fly and Beaver was with him? It was a strange question. Beaver didn't teach him anything. He was a friend, and they had a strong relationship. But Beaver hadn't taught him anything this morning.

Or had he? Gary recalled how he had the thought about jumping off a cliff, and Beaver kept him from doing it. Jumping off a cliff—it sounded ridiculous when he put it that way, but at the time, in his enthusiasm, he was considering it. He probably wouldn't have done it once he peered over the edge, but still it was helpful for Beaver to express a reasonable objection.

And that wasn't all, was it? Gary recalled how Beaver took Gary's idea and built on it productively by suggesting that Gary try jumping off the tree branch by the river. Gary's initial idea was a bad one, but Beaver took it and adjusted it and turned it into a good idea. It was much safer to jump in the river. Gary wrote down this sentence and thought about it:

The right relationships
lead to better results.

Gary never thought about it quite that way before. His relationship with Beaver was helpful for the results Gary was trying to achieve. Gary wondered whether other relationships of his could be helpful in this way too. That made him wonder about what he was doing, whether *he* was actively helping others toward their goals too.

Looking again at what he wrote, Gary wondered how he came to have such a strong relationship with Beaver. Certainly one of the reasons was that Beaver took such a sincere and supportive interest in what mattered to Gary. For instance, Beaver seemed to take as much interest in Gary's goal to fly as Gary did himself. Beaver took interest, but he went beyond that. Beaver took interest and acted on it too. He recorded these thoughts:

Build relationships by
learning what matters most to
others and taking action.

Gary thought about how it was great to have Beaver helping him to achieve his goal. It was more fun chasing his dream of flying with Beaver's support. Gary also recalled how Beaver knew just what to say to make Gary laugh when Gary took himself too seriously.

But there was more to it than Beaver just being there when times were good. Beaver was also there when times were tough. Just like today. Beaver had been there through effort and failure many times over the years they had known each other. That meant a lot to Gary in a way he hadn't fully appreciated before.

He and Beaver had been through challenges, but looking back, they didn't seem so bad. That was because Gary thought more about how they had pulled through than about how hard it was at the time.

Gary realized there was learning in that too. He wrote down:

Strong relationships make success more enjoyable and hardship more endurable.

As Gary looked at that statement, he thought about how useful that knowledge could be going forward. He would look for opportunities to acknowledge the successes of people he knew. He would also carry more optimism into future challenges, knowing that if he faced them with others, or if he helped others with theirs, the end would be better no matter what.

There was something else too. Gary realized that these statements he was writing, they weren't just about this morning with Beaver. Following the advice that Old Fish gave him seemed to be leading to principles that could apply not only this morning but always. He could use each of these principles even more intentionally and benefit even more from them.

Others in his set of relationships would gain too. They would benefit just the way Gary himself was benefiting from meeting Old Fish, whom he didn't even know a few minutes before. But because Gary knew Beaver, who in turn connected Gary with Old Fish, all sorts of interesting realizations were coming.

Without Beaver's help, for example, Gary would not have known to try to meet Old Fish. Had he known the value of trying, he would have been willing to put forth a great amount of effort to meet Old Fish. And yet, without any effort on his part, and very little on Beaver's, new relationships were developing, and new value was emerging, and no doubt there was more to come. Gary wrote:

The value in relationships
is boundless because
each one connects you with
untold others.

# Chapter III:
## *Bigger, Stronger, Faster*

GARY kept walking and thinking about this when suddenly he heard a noise. Someone was moaning in pain. He walked toward the sound and came into a clearing. In front of him, he saw a horse lying on his side.

"Are you okay?" Gary asked.

Horse looked left and right. "Who said that?"

"Over here," Gary said. Horse still couldn't see him, so Gary grabbed a leaf and waved it over his head. "Down here!"

"Oh, there you are," said Horse. He moaned in pain again. "I've twisted my knee." Horse nodded his head toward his front left leg. "It hurts so much I can't get up and walk. I can't seem to put any weight on it."

He tried to get up. He rolled on his stomach and raised himself up on his three healthy legs, but when he put the injured leg down and tried to walk, he winced again and lay down on his side.

Gary felt terrible for Horse. He was obviously in a lot of pain. He wondered if there were others around who were big enough to pick Horse up. He didn't see anyone.

As he looked for a big animal, Gary remembered his instructions from Old Fish. Horse was certainly bigger, stronger, and faster—a hundred times that and more. Gary thought it was too bad he couldn't follow the advice from Old Fish now because Horse was in so much need. Lifting Horse seemed even more impossible than flying.

Gary felt helpless, and he hated the feeling. What could he do?

Then he thought again about what Old Fish had said. Old Fish said Gary should "help" someone like Horse. But helping Horse didn't mean that he had to do the lifting himself. Was there something else he could do to help?

Gary thought more about the situation, and in a burst of insight, he realized that a bigger animal wouldn't solve the problem anyway. The problem was not how to lift Horse up. With some effort, Horse could get up already. He had done so just a minute ago.

So if lifting Horse wasn't the real problem, what was? What Horse needed to do was to walk, and that meant putting weight on his leg. That was the problem: being able to put weight on his leg.

If that was the problem, then what was the solution? Horse's injured leg needs to heal, thought Gary, and so his leg needs to be supported enough so Horse can put weight on it. The solution is keeping the leg straight and supported so Horse wouldn't bend it or twist it accidentally while it was healing.

Gary thought about how this might be done, and he had an insight. Gary remembered the sketch he had made in the sand earlier that morning. Rather than carrying one feather in each hand, he was going to strap them to his arms for additional steadiness and support.

If he could do that to his arm, couldn't he do something similar to Horse's leg?

With Beaver's help, Gary knew he could put a splint on Horse's leg. Gary knew of Beaver's skill working with wood because of the dam he was building in the river nearby. With a strong and sturdy splint, Horse would be able to walk. He would need to be careful for a few weeks and go slowly, but eventually the leg would get stronger, and Horse would be back to normal.

Gary promised Horse he would return, and he went to find Beaver to help.

Together they came back to the clearing where the Horse lay and found some fallen tree branches of the right size and strength. Working together, they put them on either side of Horse's injured leg and secured them with vines.

Horse got up again and very lightly put weight on his injured leg. He winced, but he stayed up and didn't collapse.

He cautiously took a small step. Again he winced, but again he didn't fall. "It hurts a bit, but it's bearable. I feel clumsy too, but I think it's going to work," said Horse.

Horse took a step, and then another. He limped awkwardly, but he stayed up, and he kept moving. Beaver and Gary clapped and cheered.

Horse smiled and thanked them both. "I can't tell you how important this is to me. Because of your help, I'll be able to get back to my normal life and do my work."

"I'm glad I could help," said Beaver. "And speaking of work, I better get back to my dam. I want to sturdy it up a bit more today." Horse thanked Beaver again, saying he hoped they could stay in touch.

"Gary, my new friend," said Horse after Beaver left, "I hope I can do something soon to return your kindness."

Gary said it was good of him to offer, but helping Horse required no repayment. "I didn't do it to get anything in return. I helped you because I could. And it felt good to do it."

Horse hobbled around some more and found the splint was working quite well. He asked Gary how he came up with the idea. Gary said he had been working on another project, and he saw a connection between that and Horse's injury.

"What's the other project?" asked Horse.

"I'd rather not say. You'll laugh if I tell you," said Gary.

Horse insisted, so Gary told him about wanting to fly. He paused and waited for Horse to laugh. But Horse didn't laugh. So Gary looked for a sign that Horse was keeping his ridicule under control. He stared at Horse intently.

"Why are you looking at me so strangely?" Horse asked.

"Why *aren't* you looking at *me* strangely?" said Gary.

"Because I'm impressed," said Horse.

"You are?" asked Gary. "You don't think it's ridiculous that I want to fly?"

"Just because something hasn't been done, and even if it can't be done, doesn't make it ridiculous," said Horse.

"Ah, so you don't think I can do it?" asked Gary.

Horse asked Gary if he had flown yet. Gary said technically he almost did.

"It was more of a fall than a flight, though I did drop through a few feet of air," said Gary.

"That's a start," said Horse.

"But then I swam through a few feet of water. It would be more convenient if my dream was paddling instead of flying."

Horse said, "Sometimes our dreams choose us as much as we choose them, and there's nothing to do but accept them and keep trying." He asked Gary why he wanted to fly, and Gary said he'd love to feel it, the freedom of it. And he'd love to see what things look like from so far up.

Horse nodded and said, "You know what, Gary? I think you're going to do it."

"Really?" asked Gary.

"Really," said Horse. "And I think you'll do it soon."

Gary thanked him for the vote of confidence. Horse said, "I'd like to meet with you again, Gary. How about tomorrow, same time, same place?"

Gary agreed, and he found himself with much to think about on his walk home. How extraordinary it was that he was able to do what Old Fish asked him to do, helping someone bigger, stronger, and faster. A horse! They don't come much bigger, stronger, and faster than that. Gary took a note:

Anyone can build relationships because anyone can add value in some way to just about anyone else.

It's just a matter of finding out what they need.

Horse's need was obvious because of his injury. Sometimes the needs of others that will provide those relationship-building starting points will be clearly apparent. In other cases, it might take some thought and conversation to find out.

Gary also thought about the unexpected nature of his encounter with Horse and the exciting new relationship that had come from it. It all happened so suddenly. Gary could not have anticipated the start of such an interesting new relationship. Gary wanted to capture this point too, knowing that if it happened today with Horse, it might happen again with others:

The opportunity to build
a life-changing relationship
can happen anytime.

The opportunity can come
in a new relationship
or as a defining moment
in an existing relationship.

There was one more thing. It was with Beaver's help that Gary made the splint that enabled Horse to walk. Because he knew Beaver, he was able to ask him to help Horse too. Gary's ability to help was multiplied by Beaver's capability just because Beaver was his friend. Gary wrote this down:

Relationships
are value multipliers.

They multiply your ability
to add and receive value
by the total of the
knowledge and abilities of
everyone you know.

## Chapter IV:
## Up, Up, Another Way

THE next morning, Gary came back to the clearing. Horse was still limping and moving carefully, but he looked a little better than he did the day before. Gary asked Horse how he felt, and he said he was improving, one step at a time.

"But I didn't ask you here for a progress check, Gary," said Horse.

"What did you have in mind?" asked Gary.

Horse said something, but Gary missed it, distracted instinctively by a movement above him. Gary squinted and looked up. A small movement caught his eye. There was a small spot in the sky, but it was getting bigger and bigger. It was coming straight down out of the sky toward where he stood.

Was it a rock? No, Gary realized, seized by panic. It wasn't a rock. It was a hawk in a full speed dive! It wasn't just flying; it was attacking.

Gary yelled in fear and ran for cover behind a boulder, afraid the hawk had spotted him and was going to swoop down to eat him.

The hawk spread its wings and pulled out of its dive fifty feet above the ground. Then it turned and began a slow glide down toward Horse. Then, flaring up with two quick flaps of its wings, the hawk landed lightly on Horse's back.

Horse looked left and right and asked Gary where he went. He saw Gary's head poke out carefully from behind the boulder. "Don't worry, Gary," said Horse. "Hawk is my friend."

"That's right," said Hawk. "I only want to eat you. I mean, meet you."

Gary flinched.

"She's just joking, Gary," said Horse.

Horse introduced Gary to his friend Hawk. She apologized for her dramatic arrival and said she had very much been looking forward to meeting Gary. "Horse told me all about how you came up with the way to heal him and how you got one of your friends to help make the splint. That was very generous of you and very impressive."

Gary said, "I don't know if it's all that grand. It just seemed like the right thing to do."

"It was a terrific thing to do, and that's not all I know about you," said Hawk. "Horse told me something else too."

"What's that?" asked Gary.

"He told me you want to fly," said Hawk. Gary told her that, yes, more than anything, and for as long as he could remember, he had wanted to fly.

"In that case," Hawk said, "today is a day you'll never forget. Today is the day you do it. Would you like me to take you up in the air and fly?"

Gary opened his mouth to shout yes, but no words came out. He moved his lips, but the sound was still missing. So he just nodded vigorously. His voice finally caught up with his thoughts. "Yes, yes, yes! Would you? Could I?"

Hawk hopped down off Horse's back onto the ground next to Gary. "Absolutely," she said.

Hawk spread her wings wide and motioned for Gary to come toward her feet. She opened one of her claws and said, "I'll hold you." Gary touched one of Hawk's claw tips gingerly with his paw and quickly pulled it back. "Very sharp!" he said.

"And very strong," she said, "so I'll keep you secure. And don't worry about the tips. I won't poke you with them." She held him firmly but comfortably under his two little arms. "Ready, Gary?"

"I've been ready for years," he said. "Let's do it!"

Hawk bent her knees and spread her wings. Then she sprung up with a strong jump, flapped her wings, and they were off.

Gary was more scared than he had ever been in his life. And more excited too. They lurched upward faster than Gary had ever moved in any direction, and he felt his entire body sink down as if he had gained three times his weight. In a moment, they passed over Horse's head. Horse smiled and reared up on his hind legs and said, "Go Gary, go!"

The next moment, they were clearing the treetops. Gary was amazed at their speed. They kept climbing in an upward spiral, and Gary looked down to see his friend Horse growing smaller and smaller. As he looked down, Horse appeared to shrink to the size of a gopher, then smaller still.

Gary noticed he wasn't breathing. Wasn't there air up here? He panicked a moment but then realized that he had forgotten to breathe. Since the first upward jerk at takeoff, he had held his breath. Now he made himself breathe again and felt relieved.

As they finished their steep climb and flattened out their path of flight, Gary's body started to feel normal again. But nothing else was normal anymore. The whole world around him had changed. The view was incredible. He didn't realize it was possible to see so much all at once. He took as much ground into view in a moment as would take him days to walk across. And though the air rushed by his face as fast as it does in a storm, still everything seemed calm around him as they effortlessly glided along. It was amazing.

Hawk asked him, "How do you feel, Gary? Are you okay?"

Gary said, "This feels fantastic, absolutely fantastic. But I'm afraid of falling." He was holding tightly to Hawk's talons, as if he might fall. Hawk reassured him that she had a good firm hold on him, and she wouldn't let go.

Gary tried loosening his grip, first a little, then altogether. Confident he was still okay, he held out his arms in front of him as if he were flying under his own power. He felt so free.

Hawk told Gary to point his arms in the direction he wanted to go, and she would fly by his direction. And so Gary angled his arms this way and that, and they gracefully turned with each new movement.

Hawk asked him, "Would you like to do some maneuvers?"

"Sure, like what?" asked Gary.

"Like this!" Hawk said. In a moment, Gary's view changed abruptly. He had been looking down at the trees, but suddenly the trees fell downward out of his view and the horizon rose. Then the horizon dropped, and all Gary saw were clouds and blue sky. Just as fast, the horizon came back but flipped upside down. Gary shook his head, trying to sort it out. But things kept changing, and suddenly he saw the trees beneath him again.

"Are you still with me, Gary?" asked Hawk. Gary was dizzy, but he realized that Hawk had flown straight up and twisted backward in the air, turning a full upside-down loop.

"That was great. Can we do another maneuver?" Gary asked.

"Sure," said Hawk. They flew straight toward a tree, gaining speed. It looked as if they were going to run straight into it.

At the last moment, Hawk turned sideways, and they veered sharply, whizzing narrowly between two branches.

"Wow!" Gary exclaimed, amazed at the feeling of flying and doing these maneuvers. He had thought about flying for so long and in his imagination had taken many flights. *Actually* flying—doing it for real—turned out to be so much better.

Gary thought about how relationships expanded reality for him. With a simple intention of helping Horse, suddenly things he could only dream about were happening. He had used hard work and will power to try to achieve his goal of flying and hadn't got close to doing it. He made a mental note to write down another principle:

Relationships expand what is possible. They can make dreams become real.

Gary realized that he was still learning from the suggestion Old Fish had given him. Now he was learning about the power of relationships from Hawk, whom he had met only a few minutes before. It was amazing for Gary to consider how someone he didn't even know well was giving him the gift of his life's dream—all because of what he and Beaver had done for Horse and ultimately because Old Fish had pointed him toward relationship-building principles. He would certainly have plenty to tell Old Fish when he got back.

Gary wondered if flying was still fun for Hawk too, especially because she had been doing it for so long.

"Never," said Hawk when he asked her. "Flying is a great goal to have, Gary, because it's about freedom. If you have your sights on things that make you feel free, then you'll always be on track. It doesn't have to be flying. It's whatever makes you feel like you're doing something that frees the real you. Maybe that's why flying never gets old for me. I do it every day, and every day I'm excited about flying more. I should tell you also that it thrills me to help you reach your dream and to help someone who helped my friend Horse."

Gary thought about how Hawk did both what she loved and what she did so well. It was passion aligned with skill that enabled her to give Gary the gift of flight, the fulfillment of a life's dream. What if this was the basis on which Gary interacted with others more often?

He could look for opportunities where his passion and skill could add value to others. After all, even though he didn't realize it at the time, isn't that exactly what he did with Horse? He loved working on solving problems, and Beaver loved to construct things. What they did was a natural use of the talents they enjoyed, and Horse benefited from it too. Gary wanted to remember that point:

To build strong relationships with others, first build one with yourself:

Find your own strengths and continue building on them.

As he and Hawk continued to glide through the air, Gary thought about the progress of his relationships. He thought about Beaver, whom he had known a long time, and about Horse, whom he had known a short time, and finally about Hawk, whom he has known only a few minutes.

All three of those relationships were growing, and it seemed to Gary that all his relationships got stronger by giving, by adding value. It occurred to him there was a broader lesson that unified everything he had discovered about relationships in the last two days:

To build relationships,
new ones or old ones,
learn what others need
and help them get it.

Gary began to grasp how the chain of value continues to grow. Hawk derived enjoyment from doing a favor for Horse and helping Gary—doing what she loved and sharing it with him. And he in turn was having the time of his life. And who knew what additional value might come from all of this?

In proportion to the great value that had been created over the past day, Gary also noticed paradoxically how little effort was involved for each of those who had given to others to keep this chain of value growing. Gary had done something that was easy for him to do, giving Horse the idea for supporting his leg and asking his friend Beaver to help. It was almost effortless. Building the splint was fun and easy for him and Beaver to do. It was easy for Horse to ask Hawk for a favor, and it was easy for Hawk to help Gary fly.

Through a few easy steps taken by others, Gary got to do something that was impossible for him to do with all the effort he could possibly muster by himself. He thought about the principle behind this insight:

Even small steps and little efforts can be significantly relationship building and value producing.

Gary had another thought. Helping Horse had felt more like fun than effort. It was a contribution, not an investment. He did it because it was right, not because it would pay off. What if Horse had done nothing for him in return? He wouldn't have minded, not one bit. He wouldn't have given it a thought. And he was looking forward to meeting Horse again anyway without expectations. He simply took steps to help.

He thought more of how Horse had responded by taking an interest in him. There was wisdom in that too. Horse had found out what mattered to Gary and said that he wanted to stay in touch with him. From the beginning, Horse acted as if he was going to be a long-time acquaintance, maybe even a long-time trusted friend.

It was different from Gary's usual first meetings with others, and it made a difference. Imagine if he had put only half the splint on horse's leg, then asked, "Well, Horse, what will you do for me in return?" That would be ridiculous. And he would feel terrible.

But Gary realized that in a lot of cases, he approached relationships with a wait and see attitude. He realized how well it worked to start relationships as if they would last a long time, instead of being so guarded. Horse's injury had forced him to set those normal responses aside, and Horse set them aside too.

And it worked better for both of them, accelerating the development of their relationship. They got straight to what mattered with each other, and they quickly formed the type of bond that normally took him years to establish. Gary felt it was a powerful insight:

Bring a long-term perspective
to your relationships,
even your new ones.

Act as if the other person
will be connected with you
for a long time to come.

It brings out the best
in both of you.

It occurred to Gary that there was another important point too. In addition to being aware of what others needed in order to add value to them, he needed to be clear about his own wants and goals. He had to let others know about his goals to enable them to help him achieve them. Horse would not have been able to ask Hawk to help Gary if Horse had not found out that Gary wanted to fly.

Horse almost didn't find out, only because Gary felt bashful at first about sharing his dream. What Gary learned is that you can't be too humble or shy or embarrassed about what you're working toward. You need to be clear about it, and you need to let others know. He must remember that others tend to want to be helpful, just as Gary himself wants to be.

Horse's need was clearly visible because he was injured and could not move. But most others, most of the time, have needs and wants that aren't obvious, just as Gary's dream wasn't apparent to Horse until he described it. It made Gary wonder how often others do not make requests because they think it will be futile or because they are too prideful or because they fear rejection. So Gary made a mental note:

Clarify what you're working
toward and let others know.

That enables them
to help you, just as you want
to help them.

"Gary . . . Gary?" It was Hawk trying to get his attention. Gary realized that he had drifted deep into thought. The feeling and perspective of flying had gotten his mind so engaged he hadn't even heard Hawk calling him. Hawk asked him if there was anywhere else he wanted to go.

Gary thought about the last few principles he had clarified for himself, and so in response, he decided to ask Hawk a question. "Is there anything you need to do? Anywhere you'd like to go?"

Hawk said no; she had nothing to do for the moment, though she would need to go check in on her children a little later. Gary surmised that Hawk's children must be very important to her, so he followed his own thinking about the importance of finding out about what matters most to others. Gary said. "Let's go now. I'd love to meet them."

Soon they came to a large tree, and near the top was Hawk's nest. They flew over it, and Gary saw three little baby hawks inside. He was surprised to see that they were his size, even a bit smaller. Hawk set Gary down in the nest and introduced him. "Gary, these little rascals are the light of my life. They mean everything to me. Every day I think about how to raise them well and get them ready to lead their lives when they leave the nest. And nothing means more to me than the look in their eyes when I've done something to make them happy."

At that moment, Gary knew what Old Fish meant the day before. Gary had asked him what he should do after he fulfilled the task Old Fish gave him. Old Fish said, "You'll know what to do." And now he did. He needed to go back to Old Fish to do it.

## Chapter V:
## Old Knowledge, New Value

AFTER Hawk made sure her children had everything they needed, they flew back to the clearing. Horse was excited to see Gary and listened eagerly as Gary described all he had done and seen.

Gary thanked Hawk, who asked if Gary would like to fly again.

"Absolutely!" said Gary.

"Great. In the morning, I'll be flying by South Canyon to get food for my children, but I'll be back by this time in the afternoon," said Hawk.

"Terrific, I'll see you then," said Gary.

Gary went back to the river, met up with Beaver along the way, and told him about his exciting day. Then he found Old Fish and told him he thought he knew what Old Fish had in mind last time they spoke.

"Oh really?" Old Fish asked. "What's that?"

"You wanted me to come back and tell you what I've learned. To let you know I've gained from the experience because that's valuable to you. Because you're older and have learned much over the years, you get satisfaction from sharing your knowledge and knowing it has an impact."

"I learned a lot about how to build relationships and the power that comes from that. One of the things I learned is that it's important to find what the other person values and try to help them achieve it. You and I have a relationship, and you knew right from the beginning something very important to me—flying. You also knew something I didn't at the time, how much I could learn and gain from relationship building. And so you pointed me in that direction. What I didn't know then, but do now, is the value my journey has for you. You gained too. Not in the same way I did but in the feeling that comes from helping someone else grow."

"You're right, Gary. I'm an older guy, 'long in the fin' as they say, and it gives me great satisfaction to share some of what I've learned with others younger than me. Tell me what else you learned."

So Gary told Old Fish about the day's events and all the principles he had learned about building relationships. Gary also had a question for Old Fish. He wondered how Old Fish could have known that Gary would come across Horse when he was injured and how that would lead to Hawk taking him in the air. "You're way over here in the water, far from where all this happened. How could you possibly know how it would all work ahead of time?" Gary asked.

"I didn't know. I couldn't have foreseen the specific steps that stood between your dream of flying and you actually doing it," replied Old Fish. "I didn't know *how* you would. I only knew that you *could*. And that's another power of relationships—they do the work of sorting out seemingly impossible paths. I knew you could fly, somehow, someway, so it was a matter of helping your relationship building skills help you get there."

Gary saw another lesson in what Old Fish just said:

Relationships sort out seemingly impossible paths between where you are and where you want to be.

He shared this with Old Fish, and as he did, he also realized how much he had found on the way to achieving his dream. "It's great to have Horse and Hawk as new friends," said Gary. "In fact, I'm meeting Hawk tomorrow for another flight. But before I go, I have another question for you. Why did you suggest I do a favor for someone bigger, stronger, and faster, instead of simply telling me directly about these relationship building principles?"

"There's an old saying in the sea," replied Old Fish, "if you don't swim it, you don't know it. The more that these truths come from your own experience, the more useful they will be to you. And now that you know them, the next challenge will be putting them consistently into action. As we also say in the sea: Don't just say it, swim it."

It occurred to Gary that Old Fish himself had helped someone bigger, stronger, and faster by giving advice to Gary. Old Fish had set Gary on a path that resulted in Horse getting the help that he needed. If one were to give full credit for Horse's recovery, Old Fish had a hand in it. A fin, anyway.

So Old Fish, through his advice, had done exactly what he asked Gary to do. Gary shook his head, sorting it all out. A few simple truths played out with lots of complexity.

Gary told Old Fish what he was thinking, how there was something expansive about relationship building that Gary hadn't appreciated before. There's an interconnected quality to the principles. Principles start working together even if only one person sets them in motion. And with a little intention and effort, the relationship-building principles took on a life and momentum of their own, spreading value back and forth in all directions.

"That's right," said Old Fish. "You can start with any one of the principles. They all relate and reinforce one another. Put one into action, and the rest come more naturally. If you take the first step, it's a law of nature that they will take hold with someone. They will take hold and be reciprocated. Not everyone will respond immediately. Not everyone will respond favorably. But many will, and many of those who don't respond at first will come around. Make the first move—and make it again and make it again."

Gary realized he had another lesson to note:

Any relationship-building action supports all others and makes them come easier.

Take the first step, and it will often be reciprocated.

They talked about how it's not that you have to do a favor only for someone bigger, stronger, and faster. The point is simply looking for opportunities to add value and that you can do it for anyone. Everyone is reaching for something, no matter how talented they are. So anyone can benefit from relationship building.

And it is so much the better if you can help someone with different strengths than you have because that relationship will likely connect you to others who have different strengths, skills, talent, knowledge, and experience. The more you connect with people with differences, the more those strengths become accessible. If you have a trusted friend with strengths you lack, and he is willing to act on your behalf, those strengths are as good as your own. Just in the way that Gary's talent at solving problems was put into action for Horse.

And it doesn't stop there: the strengths of other people whom you know come into play as well. Horse helped Gary by calling on the special talent of Hawk. Gary helped Horse by calling on Beaver's skill. And Beaver helped Gary by introducing him to Old Fish.

"And Beaver helped me," said Old Fish, "by introducing me to you."

"By enabling you to share your learning with me," said Gary.

"Exactly right. But that's not all. There's something else I've just learned from you, Gary, something else I've wanted to do, and now I know how I can do it."

"Really?" asked Gary. "What's that?"

"Come back tomorrow, and I'll show you," said Old Fish. And with that, he swam off, waving a fin goodbye.

## Chapter VI:
## A Favor More Than Returned

GARY awoke the next morning looking forward to the events of the day. He was excited about flying again. He was also excited to learn more about his new friends Old Fish, Horse, and Hawk.

This was something else he was learning about building relationships—that there was more at work than the exchange of value back and forth. Because of his new approach to relationships, Gary was seeing others at their best. When someone like Hawk was sharing what she loved to do with Gary, she was enthused and fun to be with.

Likewise when Beaver was helping to build the splint for Horse, Beaver was doing something he loved and did well, and he was able to do it in a way that was a positive challenge for him and appreciated by others.

Thus, Gary realized that helping others do what they are good at doing and love to do in a way that is valued by someone else is inherently relationship building and creates more enjoyment on both sides of the relationship. Gary made a note:

Strive to help others
be at their best
by helping them do what they
do well and love to do.

That creates value for
themselves and others.

Gary felt empowered by the idea that he was seeing the good side of others, not only by chance but by helping to give others the opportunity to act on their strengths and passions. He was excited about trying to do that consistently and not simply taking for granted someone else's mood or state.

Gary wondered whether he was showing his good side to others consistently. He asked himself some questions: What did he do well? What did he love to do? How could he do these things in ways that add value to others?

For him, the first thing that came to mind was solving problems. Gary loved to find solutions to challenging issues. He did it all the time in designing and building his tunnels. He had to choose the right locations, the right routes, the right connections between tunnels. And, of course, he had to find creative ways to design them so the tunnel entrances were in view of where birds liked to fly so he could easily watch them. It was creative problem solving that he used in helping Horse with his injured leg too. He resolved to be more attentive to how he could use his problem-solving skills more in the future so others could see his best self more often. To help himself remember, he wrote down the following:

Strive to be at your best consistently by doing what you love to do and doing it well.

That creates value for yourself and others.

Gary realized that by enacting relationship-building principles, he was being at his best and helping others to be at their best too. In consequence, he noticed an acceleration in the development of his relationships and the results he saw coming from them, both for himself and for others.

Gary headed toward the river to share his new thoughts with Beaver and Old Fish. When he arrived, he saw that they were already together. Gary said, "I've got something very interesting to tell you, and I'd love to hear your thoughts on it."

They didn't respond. It was as if they hadn't heard him. They seemed to be looking past him. With a dreadful look on his face, Beaver pointed behind Gary and said, "Look!" Gary turned around and gasped. There were billows of smoke on the horizon behind him. He hadn't noticed because he'd been facing the other direction all the way to the river.

Old Fish said, "I haven't seen smoke like that for many, many years."

As they watched, the smoke grew thicker and thicker. It was spreading across the horizon, and it was advancing toward them too. With dread in his voice, Gary said, "It's coming this way."

Old Fish said, "The last time the smoke was this bad was the time of the Great Fire when everything was burned right up to the riverbank."

"The little hawks!" exclaimed Gary. "They're in danger. And Hawk is too far away this morning, flying over South Canyon. She won't see the smoke from there, and so she won't be able to save them in time. The fire will reach their tree. They can't fly yet. They're trapped!"

"We've got to try to help, but what can we do?" asked Beaver.

"I have an idea," said Gary. "Come with me, Beaver, hurry!" They ran toward Hawk's nest.

When they arrived, Gary told Beaver his plan. They found a tree near Hawk's tree that was close enough to lean against it, if it were cut at the base. Gary explained that Beaver could cut away at the trunk of the tree so that it could fall slowly into the tree with Hawk's nest in it.

"If you can cut into a tree so it will fall against this one, it can make a ramp for the little hawks, and I'll go up and guide them down." Beaver set about chewing a wedge low in the trunk on the side facing the tree with Hawk's nest at the top.

Beaver chewed as fast as he could while the smoke around him billowed and the heat grew intense. "Gary, I'll climb up and get them," said Beaver. "I can carry them behind me on my paddle."

Gary said, "That's a great idea, Beaver. I'll come with you because they know me. They might be too frightened to go with a stranger."

"Wait! What about Horse?" Gary asked.

"What do you mean?" asked Beaver.

"The fire is coming in from all sides and advancing fast. Horse needs to get across the river too," said Gary.

"Horse swims, doesn't he?" asked Beaver.

"Usually he could. But with his hurt leg, Horse won't be able to swim across the river," said Gary. "Beaver, you've got to go back to the riverbank and build a bridge for Horse to walk across. There isn't much time. I'll take care of the little hawks. We'll meet you at the river."

"But the trees are too short," said Beaver. "They won't reach the whole way."

Gary thought quickly. "You can cut some that will rest against your dam from one side of the river. And from the other riverbank, you can cut more that will rest against your dam on the other side. That will make a bridge that will go all the way across. Horse will be able to get to safety, and the little Hawks and I can cross this way too. But you have to go quickly."

"I'm on it," said Beaver, hurrying back toward the river.

Gary began making his way up the inclined log. As he neared the top, he could see that it wouldn't be long before the flames reached the tree.

Gary arrived at the nest and looked down into it. The little hawks looked scared, but then they recognized him. He told them to stay calm and follow him to a place where they would be safe, and he promised to reunite them with their mother. Because they could not yet fly, he had to make sure they didn't slip or lose their balance coming down the steeply inclined tree. If they fell at this point, they would be severely injured or worse.

He set them in a line and had each grab another's tail to stay steady. The one in front grabbed Gary's tail. He told them to be careful as they walked steadily and slowly down the inclined tree.

Gary kept turning back to check on them, and each time he did, he saw the flames approaching closer. Now he saw the tree that Hawk's nest was in had caught on fire. "Don't look back," he told the little Hawks, concerned that they might panic. "Just keep going. You're doing fine." By the time they got to the bottom of the inclined log, the tree with their nest had burned all the way to the top, and Gary saw Hawk's nest burst into flame. All four of them stepped off the log just as the tree with their nest gave way and the inclined log came crashing down. "Keep following me," Gary encouraged. They narrowly missed disaster, just managing to stay ahead of the flames.

Back at the riverbank, Beaver told Horse and Old Fish about Gary's plan. Beaver felled two trees side by side that reached his dam. Horse wanted to wait for Gary and the little Hawks, but Beaver urged him on, saying he could swim back over to look for them after Horse was safely across. Horse hobbled across to Beaver's dam awkwardly but successfully. Beaver felled two other trees in similar fashion from the bank on the other side of the river, allowing Horse to walk the rest of the way across the river.

Horse, Beaver, and Old Fish looked intently across the river. Their concern grew with each passing minute with no sign of Gary and the little hawks. Beaver swam to the other side to look more closely, but it was so hot near the shoreline he couldn't stay close for long. Several times, he approached the shore and called for Gary but heard nothing in reply. He came back to Horse and Old Fish and shook his head gravely. They all waited anxiously, hoping against hope to see their friends.

Suddenly they heard a loud cry in the air behind them, and they turned to see Hawk flying down toward them. They told her that Gary and her children were still on the other side. Hawk flew to look for them, circling around the spot where her nest used to be, then flying up and down the riverbank calling for them desperately.

The fire advanced through the trees and brushed up to the river's edge where it began to die down at last. Still there was no sign of Gary and the little ones. With a heavy heart, Hawk flew to her companions on the other side of the river.

They could tell Hawk had terrible news to deliver. She landed and was about to speak when Horse interrupted. "Wait, what's that?"

Horse pointed toward the other side of the river where a small figure was climbing onto one of the logs that Beaver used to make a bridge for Horse. At first, it was one figure on the log, then there appeared a second figure, then a third, and a fourth.

Hawk turned and looked, and with her sharp eyesight, she knew immediately who it was. "It's Gary, and he's got my little ones with him!" she cried. Horse, Beaver, and Old Fish cheered; and Hawk took to the air, flying above the line of little creatures coming their way.

They couldn't imagine how Gary and the little Hawks had survived. When all of them were safely across, Gary explained what happened. After they got to the ground from Hawk's nest, Gary knew the fire would catch up to them before they could reach the river. So he took the little hawks straight to his nearest gopher hole. They were able to stay far enough down to be safe from the smoke and heat. They waited until the fire passed and then made their way down to the river.

"I'm glad your little ones weren't much older," Gary said to Hawk. "They were still small enough to fit comfortably." He patted his belly and laughed. "I'm also glad I've been getting plenty of exercise lately so that I could fit in there too."

Hawk reached back with her beak and plucked out a small tail feather. "Gary," she said, "I can never thank you enough for what you've done. I want you to know that now I consider you a member of our family." She leaned over and placed the feather behind Gary's ear. He beamed with pride. "Any time you want to fly," she said, "you just let me know. And though I'm too big to come visit you in your tunnels, you're welcome in our nest anytime."

"You'll be needing another one of those," said Beaver, and they all laughed. "I'll be happy to help build it."

"Thank you, Beaver," said Hawk. "And thank you for helping to save my children." Horse thanked Beaver and Gary too for helping him walk and building the bridge so he could escape the fire too.

Gary said, "It's getting complicated, all this thanking. It's interesting how everyone has everyone else to thank in some way just over the past couple of days. But I want everyone to know that it all came from the advice I got from Old Fish who pointed me toward putting relationship-building principles into action in the first place."

"And that reminds me," said Gary turning to Old Fish. "Wasn't there something you wanted to show me today?"

"Ah, yes," said Old Fish. He thought a moment and swam over to Beaver and whispered something in his ear. Beaver laughed and then said to Old Fish, "Of course."

"What's going on?" asked Gary. Old Fish just smiled.

He and Beaver swam out together toward the middle of the river and then swam behind a part of Beaver's dam so they were hidden from view to the others on shore.

Gary looked at Horse and Hawk and asked, "Do you know what's happening?" They shrugged and said no.

Old Fish spoke up from behind Beaver's dam. "Gary, when you told me how Hawk helped you fly, it made me think of a way I could do something fun that I've never done."

"What's that?" asked Gary.

"Water ski!" said Old Fish. That instant, Beaver came into view, swimming fast across the water. And there was Old Fish too, lying on Beaver's tail, which Beaver kept flat out on the surface of the water.

Old Fish stood up and balanced on his own tail and waved at the others on shore. "Look, no fins!" he said.

"Oh, you want to do stunts?" said Beaver. "How about a water ski jump?"

"A what?" asked Old Fish.

"This!" said Beaver as he flipped his tail upward, sending Old Fish in an arc through the air. Old Fish laughed and turned a flip, then dove into the river. He came up smiling, and he and Beaver swam over to the others.

"They say you can't teach an old dog new tricks," said Old Fish. "I don't know if that's true for dogs, but I know an old fish just learned one."

Reflecting on Old Fish's comment about his age, Gary thought about how interesting it was that there were three generations of friends gathered here, all of whom gained from the relationship-building principles. There were Hawk's children, the youngest generation. The middle generation was Gary, Horse, and Beaver. And then there was Old Fish who was older than them all but still learning new things and finding new enjoyment from his relationship building. Young and old alike came out better off from the new relationships that had been forged over the last few days. Gary wanted to remember this point, so he made a note:

No matter who you are,
no matter how strong,
smart, or old,
anyone can benefit from
relationship building.

"What are you doing there, Gary?" asked Old Fish.

"You asked me to write down the things I learned. Well, I keep learning more, so I keep writing," replied Gary.

Horse asked if he could see what Gary had written. Everyone else wanted to see it too. Gary said he would indeed show them, though he wanted to review what he had written and integrate it into a set of key points. Here's how he summarized the principles of effective relationship building:

# Building Invisible Bridges:
## Applying the Power of Professional Relationships

### Understand the Strength of Invisible Bridges
Whatever you're reaching for, the right relationships
can get you there faster, easier, and with more enjoyment.
Relationships lead to the best things in life.
Relationships are the best things in life.

### Choose Bridges to Build
Decide what you want and with whom you'd like to connect.
Find creative ways to make new connections.

### Build Your Bridges from Both Sides
Find out what others value in work and life.
Let others know what you want in work and life.

### Keep Your Bridges in Good Repair
Follow up on new connections and stay in touch with your existing ones.
Take action for the benefit of your relationships, new ones and old ones.

### Be Ready for New Bridges
Anyone can build stronger relationships at any point in their lives.
You never finish building relationships, and you can always get better.
Life-changing relationships can come anytime, anywhere. Get ready.

As Gary looked over these principles, he realized how much the group of them had built in the past two days. The result was much more than the bridge that Beaver laid across the river. They had also built relationships with one another. The relationships were like invisible bridges connecting them to one another. And once built, the bridge enabled each to cross swiftly and effortlessly with value for the other.

As Gary thought about what they had gone through to build those invisible bridges, it was a source of strength and enjoyment to him. Even with the other side of the river burned and desolate, the relationships came across the river and grew stronger in the passage.

That was another great thing about relationships: they grew stronger with exercise. It was as if they all had a new durable foundation supporting them all—invisible but solid and growing stronger by the day.

Thanks to their relationship building; they had all come through a challenging time together. The relationships he developed not only helped him achieve his goal of flying, they helped fortify them all against unexpected difficulties. They were even able to laugh and think hopefully about starting their lives again now that the fire was past.

As Gary brought his summary of relationship-building principles for the others to see, he didn't know what challenges lay ahead, but he knew they would be better equipped with the relationships they had established and their knowledge about how to build more relationships.

Gary looked forward to the future on the new side of the river.

## *After the Story:*
## A Conversation

"THE end," said Gordon. "Well, what do you think?"

"I'm like Gary at the beginning of the story," said Frank. "I work really hard and try my hardest to get things done in my operations group. But I haven't been reaching some of my goals. After the story, one thing that stands out for me is how important relationships are to getting work done well. I always thought working on relationships was just socializing and wasting time."

Sharon said, "Yes, and I always thought relationship building was so complicated. It was intimidating for me to try to say and do the right things with so many different people. Now I see that the principles are straightforward and can apply to everyone. Relationships are much more manageable to me now, and I'm excited to go build a lot more of them."

"I can relate to that," said Steve. "I could use a lot more invisible bridges. I've always thought that only certain people have the talent to build lots of relationships. Like the schmoozers from Sales. Uh, no offense to you, Rebecca."

Rebecca pretended to be mad for a moment and said, "You're about to burn an invisible bridge, Steve."

Steve said, "Actually it's partly a compliment. It seems to be easy for you to talk with others who are different from you. It's not easy for me. I've always had a hard time with it. Now I see that building a broad set of relationships is something that any of us can do, not just people like you, Rebecca, for whom it comes naturally."

"It's interesting you put it that way," said Rebecca, "because I have challenges with relationship building too. Sometimes I'm perceived as superficial, and as just trying to close deals, rather than having genuine commitment to our customers. I fight that stereotype a lot. And this story helps me see how to avoid that. I am trying to increase sales and referrals, but I want to do it in a way that builds long-lasting bridges with customers and referral partners. That will help them perceive me consistently with my intentions and will help me get the sales results I need to produce as well because they'll have good reason to trust me even more."

James said, "I've had a different hang-up about relationships at work. I always thought relationships were about politics, and I never wanted to be political. I see now that I've been confusing relationships and politics."

Gordon said, "Yes, there is part of politics that can be negative, but there's another part that's necessary for an organization to be successful. It's about working together well over time and through challenges. And that comes down to strong, healthy relationships."

Frank was whispering something to Sharon, and they both started laughing.

Gordon glanced their way, but they told him to go on. So he did. "Relationship building is at the core of performance effectiveness in any group or organization. Any kind of performance involving people working together can be enhanced through more effective relationships. It's an essential ingredient of leadership, teamwork, and sales."

Frank and Sharon started laughing again, and Gordon finished, "Better relationships can help our organization deal with change, pursue opportunities, and handle unexpected challenges more effectively, just as Gary and his friends did with the fire." Then he said, "All right, you two, what's so funny?"

"I just realized something," said James. "You're one of the characters in the story."

"Oh, really?" asked Gordon. "Which one?"

"Because you're the one who told us the story to teach us these relationship-building lessons—that makes you like Old Fish," said Frank.

"Yes," laughed Sharon. "That's what we're going to call you from now on: Old Fish Gordon."

The others laughed too, and Gordon shook his head.

Rebecca said, "I think we have something to report back to the CEO now. Why don't we propose to implement these relationship-building practices in our company?"

"Yes, and let's get Old Fish Gordon to present it," said Frank.

"I'll do it if you change my nickname," said Gordon.

"Not a chance," said Steve, "you're stuck with it. But it will help us all remember to keep putting these lessons into action."

"All right," said Gordon. "How about if we start working on these relationship-building lessons right here with each other?"

And so they did.

## The End

## *Other Ways to Build Invisible Bridges*

Contact us for:

Learning Materials for Individuals and Organizations,
Workbooks, Audio CDs, Assessments, Seminars

## The Professional Relationship Institute

310.266.1559

www.priconnect.com

info@priconnect.com

*The Professional Relationship Institute* helps individuals and
organizations increase productive results through more effective
professional relationship management.

We offer a series of products, assessments, seminars, and
coaching support to help professionals increase the
effectiveness of their professional relationships
and the size and productivity of their networks
to achieve better business, career, and personal results.

Ask us about other training materials
featuring the characters of Invisible Bridges.

## About the Authors

**J**OHN Ullmen, **Ph.D.** is known—as a speaker, consultant, and executive coach—for cutting through clutter to target the most important actions for improvement. His book *Don't Kill the Bosses: Escaping the Hierarchy Trap*, coauthored with Sam Culbert, Ph.D., is in print in several languages.

He has taught executives, managers, and graduate students from around the world in a variety of institutions, including the UCLA Anderson School of Management.

His education includes a BS in Engineering Mechanics from the United States Air Force Academy, a Master of Public Policy from Harvard University, and a Ph.D. in Organizational Behavior from UCLA.

**M**ELISSA Karz, **MBA** is a highly sought executive coach, trainer, and consultant who helps highly capable people lead more powerfully and achieve results more rapidly.

Her background combines organizational consulting with leadership development, training, and executive coaching. She earned an MBA from UCLA with emphases in human resources and organizational development.

She has been featured in the *Los Angeles Times* as well as *Fortune* magazine. Prior to beginning her coaching career, Melissa consulted with PricewaterhouseCoopers to executives of major companies in healthcare, technology, consumer products, entertainment, and real estate.

BVG